W9-AFS-758

# Euthanasia

# Critical World Issues

CRITICAL WORLD ISSUES

# Euthanasia

Steve Wise

MASON CREST
PHILADELPHIA

**Mason Crest**
450 Parkway Drive, Suite D
Broomall, PA 19008
www.masoncrest.com

©2017 by Mason Crest, an imprint of National Highlights, Inc.

Printed and bound in the United States of America.

CPSIA Compliance Information: Batch #CWI2016.
For further information, contact Mason Crest at 1-866-MCP-Book.

First printing
1 3 5 7 9 8 6 4 2

Library of Congress Cataloging-in-Publication Data

on file at the Library of Congress
ISBN: 978-1-4222-3653-6 (hc)
ISBN: 978-1-4222-8133-8 (ebook)

Critical World Issues series ISBN: 978-1-4222-3645-1

# Table of Contents

---

**KEY ICONS TO LOOK FOR:**

**Words to Understand:** These words with their easy-to-understand definitions will increase the reader's understanding of the text, while building vocabulary skills.

**Sidebars:** This boxed material within the main text allows readers to build knowledge, gain insights, explore possibilities, and broaden their perspectives by weaving together additional information to provide realistic and holistic perspectives.

**Research Projects:** Readers are pointed toward areas of further inquiry connected to each chapter. Suggestions are provided for projects that encourage deeper research and analysis.

**Text-Dependent Questions:** These questions send the reader back to the text for more careful attention to the evidence presented there.

**Series Glossary of Key Terms:** This back-of-the book glossary contains terminology used throughout this series. Words found here increase the reader's ability to read and comprehend higher-level books and articles in this field.

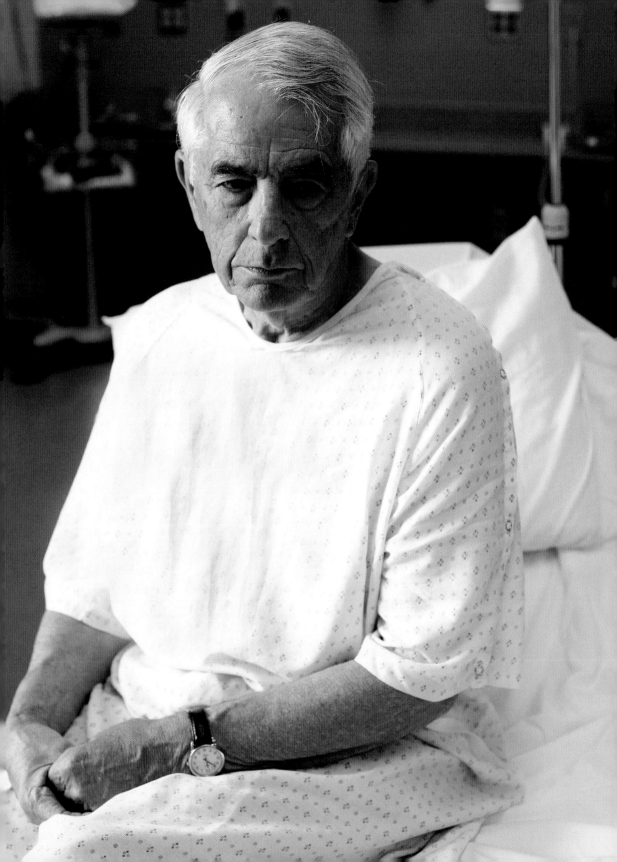

# Background of Euthanasia

Petta is 78 years old and suffers from amyotrophic lateral sclerosis (ALS), also known as Lou Gehrig's disease. This is one of the motor neuron diseases that *progressively* causes the nerve cells in the brain and spinal cord to *deteriorate*, resulting in the body's muscles growing weak and wasting away. At present, it is an incurable disease which, in most cases, leads to paralysis and death, usually from an inability to breathe. Petta is in the advanced stages of the disease and is considering the possibility of *euthanasia*, intentionally ending his life to prevent further suffering.

## Petta's Story

"My name is Petta. I was born in Denmark, although I now live in the Czech Republic. I suffer from ALS, have lost the ability

*Some people believe that a person who is incurably ill should be allowed to die a dignified death.*

to move, and need to be cared for all the time.

"I can still speak, just barely, but that ability will also go in the not-too-distant future. My doctor treats me to make sure that I am not in any great pain and to keep my mind alive, but my body feels as if it is dead. My condition has deteriorated so much that I am now past the point where I am able to physically take my own life.

"While I have any strength left at all, I am trying to talk to the members of my family about someone taking my life for me. However, my family is against euthanasia and each of them has different reasons for opposing it: My younger brother is very religious and feels that it is against the will of God as well as the teachings of the Bible. My sister, on the other hand, says that having survived a war, I should know how precious life is.

"If I were healthy, I could take my own life, but because I

 **Words to Understand in This Chapter**

**assisted suicide**—suicide with help from another person (such as a doctor) to end suffering from severe physical illness.

**deteriorate**—to become worse as time passes.

**euthanasia**—the act or practice of killing someone who is very sick or injured in order to prevent any more suffering.

**extradition**—the surrender of an alleged criminal by one authority (as a state) to another having jurisdiction to try the charge.

**living will**—a document in which one says what medical decisions should be made if they become too sick or injured to make those decisions.

**progressive**—happening or developing gradually over a period of time.

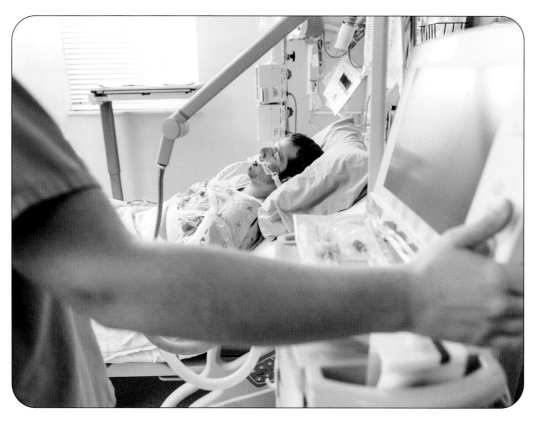

*A patient in an intensive care unit requires a massive amount of medical attention in order to stay alive.*

need help from someone, it is a big issue and against the law. As a young man, I fought to survive during World War II, but I now face a battle I cannot win and one that I no longer want to fight. Don't I have the right to die? Or should I be respecting the views of my loved ones?"

# Euthanasia Defined

The word "euthanasia" comes from two words in the Greek language: *eu* means "well" or "good," and *thanatos* means "death." In modern society, euthanasia now means much more than a "good death." It has come to mean the intentional end of a person's life to end suffering.

All people die eventually, and most die of natural causes when their bodies—due to age, illness, or injury—cease to function well enough to keep them alive. Euthanasia shortens the lifespan of a person by killing them before nature runs its course. Active euthanasia occurs by an action, such as causing a person to die by giving them a lethal injection of drugs or putting a pillow over their nose and mouth to suffocate them. Passive euthanasia happens through withholding food and water or not performing normal and necessary medical care. In the US, active euthanasia is illegal in all states, but passive euthanasia is legal.

## The Importance of Intention

Euthanasia involves deliberately performing an act or deliberately not doing something with the clear intention of causing someone's death. Without intention to kill someone, euthanasia does not occur. For example, doctors are sometimes faced with a patient who is close to death. They may decide to stop a particular treatment because it no longer has any benefit to the patient's health, or they may not start a new treatment because it will not improve the patient's conditions. Some groups argue that if these decisions result in death, they are examples of passive euthanasia. However, the general opinion is that they are part of fair medical practice that is allowed by law in most countries. Since there is no intention to kill the patient, they would not be considered euthanasia.

# 📖 Euthanasia in Ireland

The issue of the right for a person to choose the time and manner of their own death is sparking many debates and raising new questions around the world:

In 2002, mourners gathered at the funeral of Rosemary Toole Gilhooley, an Irishwoman whose death was assisted by an American minister, the Reverend George Exoo, and his assistant, Thomas McGurrin. Exoo and McGurrin traveled to Dublin, Ireland, with Toole Gilhooley, who was later found dead in the rented home where they were staying.

Exoo admitted that he and McGurrin helped set up a mechanism that would cut off Toole Gilhooley's oxygen supply. They also guided her through five practice sessions with it but claimed to only watch as she went through the procedure.

The two men faced *extradition*, or transfer from the United States back to Ireland, to face charges of assisting in a suicide, but the extradition efforts failed in 2007. The death was ruled a suicide without assistance, but there was swirling controversy because of Exoo and McGurrin's level of involvement in Toole Gillhooley's death.

More recently, a woman named Marie Fleming filed a lawsuit challenging Ireland's ban on assisted suicide. Fleming, who suffered from multiple sclerosis, wanted to make sure that her partner, Tom Curran, would not be prosecuted if he helped her to end her life. In 2013, Ireland's supreme court ruled against Fleming. However, the debate she sparked on the right to die has continued in Ireland.

*Jacques Chirac, French President from 1995 to 2007, refused an appeal by Marie Humbert in 2002 to allow her son, Vincent, to have the legal right to end his life. Vincent had lost the use of his limbs as well as his sight, speech, smell, and taste in a car crash. Before his passing away in 2003, he wrote the book* I Ask the Right to Die *with the use of his right thumb, expressing his wish to die legally.*

## The Double Effect

The double effect, or dual effect, describes how an action can have more than one effect, both good and bad. In particular, it is used to describe the practice of giving a dying patient high doses of certain powerful, painkilling drugs to control pain and ease suffering. All drugs have side effects, and in trying to control a patient's pain or another symptom, there is the chance that the side effects of the painkilling drugs may weaken the patient and bring about death more quickly. This is generally not considered euthanasia as, again, there is no deliberate intention to kill the patient, but an attempt to alleviate their suffering.

# Voluntary and Involuntary Euthanasia

Voluntary euthanasia is when the person who is killed has made a specific request for their death. In some countries where euthanasia is legal, this request has to be made a number of times by the patient over a period of time, sometimes in written form and other times verbally. In contrast, involuntary euthanasia is used to describe the killing of a person who has not clearly expressed the wish to die. Involuntary euthanasia has occurred with patients who have no ability whatsoever to communicate their wishes to caregivers, doctors, friends, or relatives. These include patients whose conditions have deteriorated to the extent that they are in a type of deep, prolonged coma that is referred to as a persistent vegetative state (PVS).

# The Difference between Euthanasia and Suicide

Euthanasia and suicide are not considered the same in the laws of most countries or in arguments about morals and ethics. Suicide is the intentional taking of one's own life. The final act does not involve anyone else helping in any way. With euthanasia, the assistance of another individual is required in taking a person's life.

In wealthier, more developed nations around the world, suicides are a significant cause of death. In the US, for example, the Centers for Disease Control report that, in 2013, there were 41,149 deaths due to suicide, which is 13 per 100,000 people. Suicide was the tenth leading cause of death of people in the US, with more deaths due to suicide than murder. The situation is similar in the United Kingdom (UK), where the Office for National Statistics reported that 6,233 people took their own lives in 2013—11.9 suicides per 100,000 people.

"It's like giving someone a loaded gun. The patient pulls the trigger, not the doctor. If the doctor sets up the needle and syringe but lets the patient push the plunger, that's assisted suicide. If the doctor pushes the plunger, it would be euthanasia."

——Dr. Jack Kevorkian, a physician famous for assisting in suicides, explaining the difference between euthanasia and assisted suicide.

## Assisted Suicide

*Assisted suicide* is when a person provides the means for someone to commit suicide but leaves the final act to the person who dies. When a doctor assists, it is known as physician-assisted suicide. The person who actually performs the final action which causes death is what separates assisted suicide from euthanasia. If the person who dies performs the last act, such as the swallowing of a lethal drug prescribed by a doctor, then it is classified as assisted suicide. But if a doctor injects a person directly with a lethal drug, then it is euthanasia. While suicide is no longer illegal in most nations, assisted suicide remains a serious crime in nearly all countries of the world.

# Living Wills

A *living will* is a legal document that sets out how someone wishes to be treated should they become unable to communicate with their doctors. Living wills cannot legally enforce euthanasia, but they can instruct a medical team not to prolong life artificially by giving antibiotic drugs to fight an infection or connecting someone to a life-support machine. Many people

*The death and funeral of a person is a traumatic time, and some people feel that the prolonged suffering of the person prior to death can add immensely to the emotional pain of those close to them.*

*Many people believe that a person making a living will is unaware of the implications of his or her decision—a decision they may be unable to reverse when the time comes.*

argue that living wills give a patient peace of mind by making their wishes clear and taking pressure away from doctors, friends, and family. Critics, however, wonder how it is possible or right to make a decision now for some unknown problem that may or may not occur at some point in the future.

# I am Young.
# Why should I be Interested?

The majority of children in more developed countries, such as the US and UK, can look forward to 80 years or more of life ahead of them. As a result, death may seem far removed as an issue of importance. Surveys reported in the book *A Right to Die* indicate that only 10 percent of 19-year-olds think of death in relation to themselves, compared to 70 percent of 65-year-olds. Yet death affects everyone, sooner or later, and many young people face it directly by being a victim of an accident, terminal illness, or through a dying friend or family member.

 # Text-Dependent Questions

1. Describe the differences between active euthanasia, passive euthanasia, voluntary euthanasia, and involuntary euthanasia.
2. Are euthanasia and assisted suicide the same? Why or why not?

 # Research Project

Using the Internet or your school library, research the topic of assisted suicide, and answer the following question: "Is there a difference between suicide and assisted suicide?"

Some claim that there is a fundamental difference. Suicide is a private act that does not involve another individual at all. Assisted suicide involves someone else helping to take a life, so another person is part of the dying process. The difference is significant and recognized by laws: suicide is not against the law in most countries, but assisted suicide is illegal in most countries. Others contend that there is no meaningful difference between suicide and assisted suicide because the end result is the same. In both cases a person wants to end their life and eventually dies. Does it really matter that someone else was involved in the process if it is the decision of the person who dies?

Write a two-page report, using data you have found in your research to support your conclusion, and present it to your class.

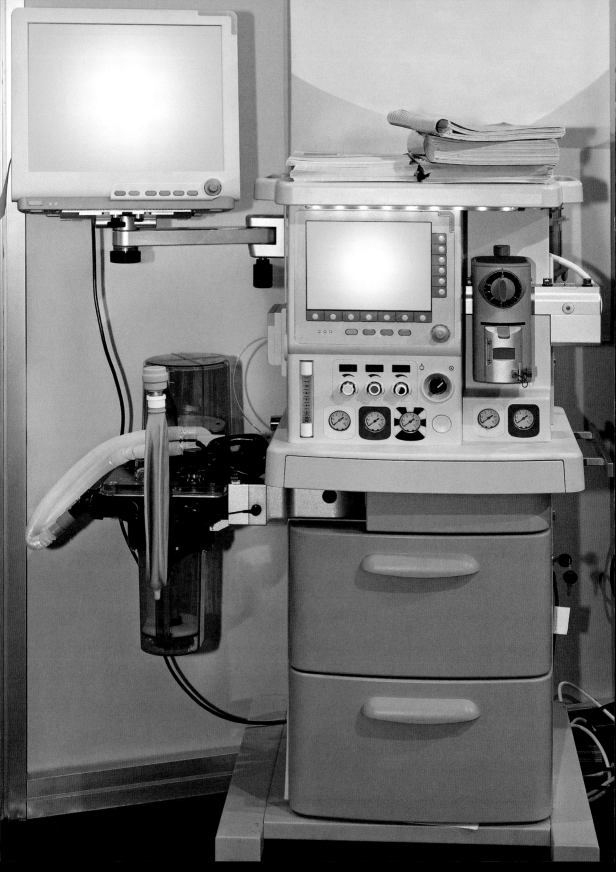

# Beginnings of the Euthanasia Debate

F ew subjects arouse more passion and stronger views than life, death, and whether people can choose between them. Debates about rights to life and death have existed since ancient times. However, it is only since the 20th century that euthanasia has truly become a major issue.

People in ancient times tended to live far shorter lives. In the past, medicine was less advanced and often unable to prolong a person's life if they were suffering serious illness or injury. To many historic peoples and cultures, death and life were woven together and part of the natural world. In the aftermath of a battle, for example, people from a number of ancient cultures killed their seriously injured comrades to give them, in their view, an honorable death.

*Modern technology, such as this life-support machine, allows us to keep people alive far beyond the time their condition would have killed them in the past.*

## Past Views about Suicide and Euthanasia

Views on suicide and euthanasia have varied throughout history. For some Ancient Greeks and Romans, both were considered acceptable. The Ancient Greek philosopher Socrates committed suicide in 399 BCE by drinking a cup of poison made from the hemlock plant. Others thought it was wrong, among them the Greek physician Hippocrates (460-377 BCE). An *oath* attributed to him is still taken by many doctors today. There are different versions, but the classic Hippocratic Oath includes concepts such as putting the good of patients above the interests of doctors and emphasizes a doctor's role in striving to preserve life.

The rise of the world's major organized religions— Christianity, Judaism, and Islam— dominated perspectives on these topics for many centuries. These three religions as well as others held human life as sacred and condemned both suicide and euthanasia. For example, the Qur'an, the chief sacred text of Islam, makes clear that life is sacred because it is only Allah ("God") who chooses how long each person should live: "No person can ever die except by Allah's leave and at an

 **Words to Understand in This Chapter**

**hospice**—a place that provides a caring environment for people who are dying.
**oath**—a formal and serious promise to tell the truth or to do something.

*A Muslim man prays at a mosque in Mali. The world's major religions include prohibitions against suicide and murder.*

appointed term." Countries whose populations followed the major religions tended to reflect this viewpoint in law, making euthanasia and suicide illegal.

# Changes in Attitudes Regarding Suicide

*Comedian and actor Robin Williams (left) with his family at a movie premiere. Williams shocked fans when he committed suicide in August 2014. His suicide was attributed to his longtime battle with depression as well as a recent diagnosis of Parkinson's disease.*

Attitudes about suicide have altered slightly in many societies in modern times. The prevalent view now is that it does no good to further punish those who are in such a state of distress, pain, or mental illness that they would try to kill themselves. Today, attempted suicide is not a crime in a large number of nations around the world, including the US and UK. Suicide is still condemned by most religions, and in a few countries, if someone commits suicide, their property can be taken by the government, or their bills can be sent to family members.

# The First Pro-Euthanasia Groups

In the early 20th century, a number of books, papers, and discussions about euthanasia started to flourish, leading to the establishment of the first organizations dedicated to the legalization of euthanasia.

The Voluntary Euthanasia Legalisation Society was founded in 1935 in the United Kingdom by Dr. C. Killick Millard. The society succeeded in introducing a bill into the British Parliament that same year, but the bill failed to become law. In 1938, the Euthanasia Society of America was formed by Charles Francis Potter in the United States. However, the attempts of these early euthanasia groups to create changes in the law and spark public debate did not succeed.

> "I will keep [the sick] from harm and injustice. I will neither give a deadly drug to anybody who asks for it, nor will I make a suggestion to this effect."
>
> —Excerpt from the Hippocratic Oath

# The T4 Program

In 1939, the Aktion ("Action") T4 program was started in Germany by the Nazi Party, which was in power at the time. It was promoted as euthanasia and mercy killing of people who had, as the Nazis described, "lives unworthy of life." Nazi officials perceived major economic benefits in ridding the state of those it claimed led "burdensome lives" and were "useless eaters." The program was first aimed at children with birth defects, but it was later extended to the incurably ill, people

*Dr. Karl Brandt at his trial for crimes against humanity after World War II. As Reich Commissioner for Sanitation and Health, he participated in the Nazi's T4 program. The International Military Tribunal found Brandt guilty of war crimes, crimes against humanity, and membership in the criminal SS organization. He was executed on June 2, 1948.*

with physical and mental disabilities, and the elderly. People who had no say in the decisions were selected by medical teams and then killed, first by starvation or injection of drugs and later in poison gas chambers. Some 70,000 innocent people were killed by the program before 1941 and an estimated 130,000 more were killed before the end of World War II (1939-1945).

# The Rising Issue of Euthanasia in Recent Years

Great advances in medical science and public health now enable people to live far longer lives on average than in the past. Life expectancy around the world has more than doubled in the last 250 years. The World Health Organization reported that the average worldwide life expectancy in 1955 was just 48 years; in 2013, that figure jumped to 71 years. A person in

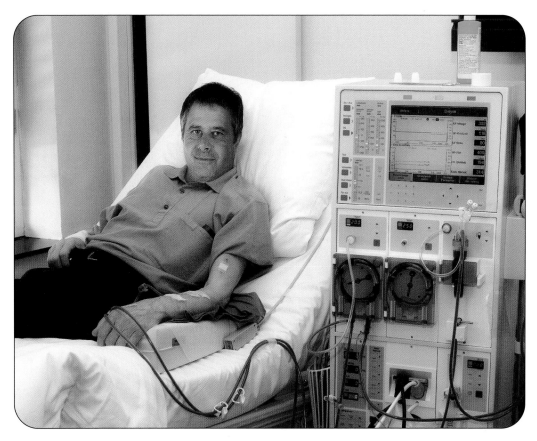

*This person is connected to a dialysis machine, which does the job his kidneys should be doing—filtering his blood. Without this machine, the patient would quickly become ill and die.*

*ER departments in modern hospitals can now treat many conditions and stop them before they can threaten a person's life.*

wealthier nations, such as Japan and Switzerland, can now expect to live for an average of 80 to 90 years.

As people live to an older age, there are increased chances that they may become exposed to certain diseases, and these can result in long, disabling, and painful illnesses. Further medical advances, including the development of medicines and machines such as respirators, now make it possible to keep people alive despite these serious illnesses. In many cases, a person would not be able to survive without the help of these medicines and machines. These developments have helped to fuel a growing euthanasia debate in countries with rapidly aging populations where health topics are of increasing interest. Some people see the prolonging of a person's life by artificial means as degrading and inhumane when the quality of life is deemed to be low.

Campaign groups on both sides have also helped to heighten the debate. Arguments have become more complex, incorporating the views of different cultures and religious perspectives in light of the aforementioned medical technology. Advances in digital communication and social media have made campaigns more effective by allowing for the instant spread of news, messages, or videos across the globe.

# The Question of an Absolute Right to Life

In 1948, the United Nations (UN), a worldwide organization of countries established after World War II, produced the Universal Declaration of Human Rights. Article 3 of the Declaration states that "Everyone has the right to life, liberty,

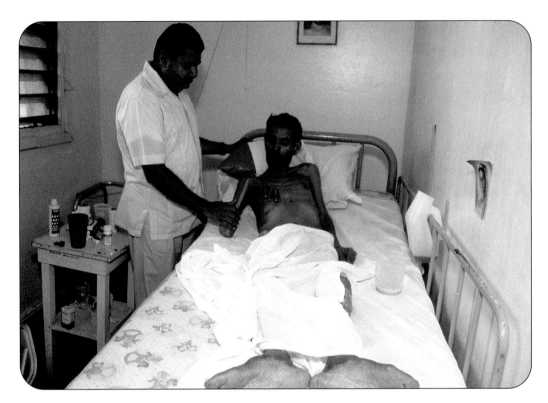

*This Honduran man is suffering from AIDS. Modern drugs, if they are available, can now prolong an AIDS suffered life far beyond what was possible twenty years ago.*

and security of person." The fundamental right to life is found in the laws and documents of many nations. In the UK, for example, the Human Rights Act of 1998 states, "Everyone's right to life shall be protected by law. No one shall be deprived of his life intentionally." The Human Rights Act does, however, make exceptions for capital punishment and self-defense.

While these and other documents appear to offer a right to life, this has a range of interpretations, and it might not be absolute in practice. The amount of medical care resources in all countries is not bottomless and often outweighed by demand from ever-increasing numbers of patients. Not every-one can receive all the medical care their condition requires, and sometimes tough decisions have to be made about where medical resources will go.

The right to life does not necessarily mean someone must be prevented from dying by all medical means for as long as possible. Patients in many countries have a right to refuse med-ical treatments and make the decision not to remain alive on life-support machines. The Toronto Right to Life Association said, "Insistence, against the patient's wishes, that death be postponed by every means available is contrary to law and

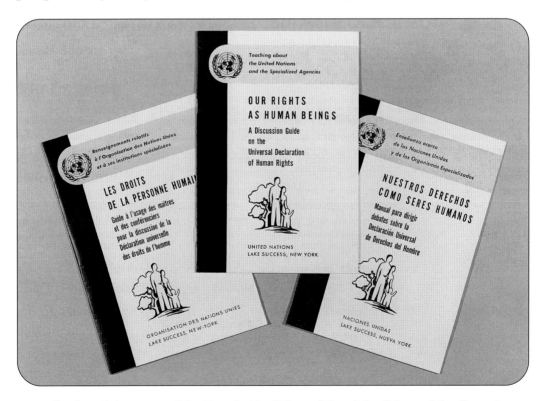

*Reproduction of the covers of the French, English, and Spanish editions of the discussion guide "Our Rights as Human Beings" published by the United Nations in 1948.*

*A poster for the Voluntary Euthanasia Society, established in 1935 in the United Kingdom. Today, this organization is known as Dignity in Dying.*

practice. It would also be cruel and inhumane. There comes a time when continued attempts to cure are not compassionate, wise, or medically sound. That's where *hospice*, including in-home hospice care, can be of such help."

 **Text-Dependent Questions**

1. How did the rise of organized religions impact views on suicide and euthanasia?
2. Provide two reasons for the euthanasia debate intensifying in recent years.

 **Research Project**

Using the Internet or your school library, research the topic of the Action T4 program, and answer the following question: "If euthanasia is legalized, could the horrors of the T4 program happen again?"

Some believe legalizing euthanasia would not lead to a repeat of the offenses of the T4 program. Hitler's program was murder, not euthanasia as it is defined today. Patients were not selected for medical or humane reasons: it was about saving money and enforcing the Nazis' political views about cleansing "undesirable" people from Germany. Today, euthanasia is defined under strict standards that include someone personally choosing to die. Others argue that making euthanasia legal could lead to abusive situations like those of the T4 program. T4 is an example of what can happen when involuntary euthanasia is backed by a government on a large scale. The danger of this occurring again concerns many opposed to legalizing any sort of euthanasia, which may be why it has not been made legal anywhere in the US.

Write a two-page report, using data you have found in your research to support your conclusion, and present it to your class.

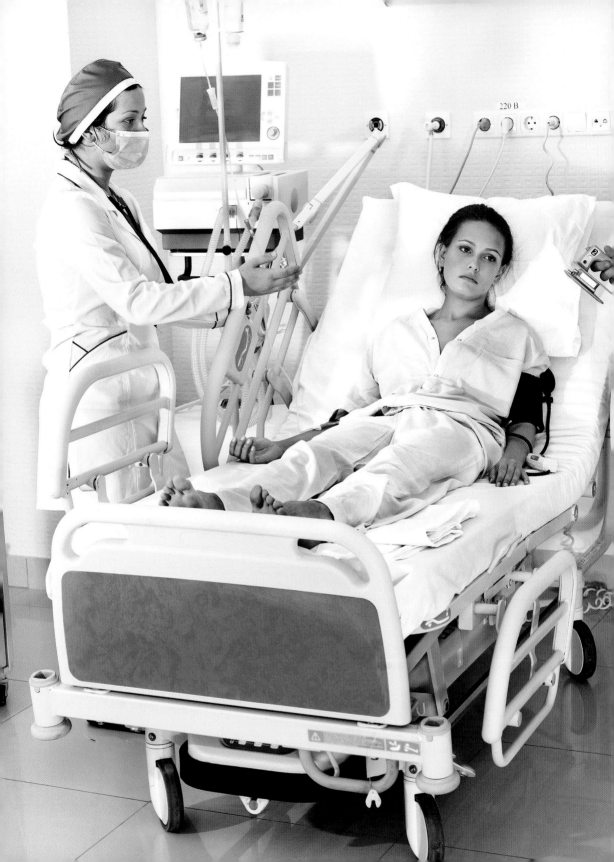

# 3

# The Arguments for Euthanasia

People wish to die for a wide range of reasons. Advocates of euthanasia feel that some of these reasons, such as being in constant, unbearable pain or being just days or weeks away from death because of an incurable illness, are valid reasons that justify euthanasia.

Most supporters of euthanasia believe that severely ill or dying patients should have the right to request that their life be ended. A frequently given example is of people suffering from a *terminal illness* for which there is no known cure. In the early stages of such an illness, people may have a relatively high quality of life. As the illness progresses, however, they may fear the suffering, dependency on others, and loss of control that their situation might bring. If someone is merely

*Supporters of euthanasia believe that allowing people to "die with dignity" is kinder than forcing them to continue their lives with suffering.*

weeks away from dying, and there is no possible cure, they contend, why can't they be given the chance to choose the exact moment and manner of their death?

## The Argument of Showing Mercy

Euthanasia cases are sometimes called "mercy killings" in the media—a name that highlights an important point of view. We live in a civilized society where every effort is made to provide as high a quality of life to as many people as possible. Should we not show mercy to help sick people avoid great suffering, and give them as peaceful a death as is possible?

Critics of euthanasia maintain that advances in painkilling medicine mean that most patients, as many as 95 percent, do not suffer pain, but euthanasia activists counter by asking about the remaining 5 percent, some of whom may be in absolute agony. Is it acceptable in a civilized society to force people who want to die to stay alive in great pain or distress?

 **Words to Understand in This Chapter**

**alleviate**—to reduce the pain or trouble of (something): to make (something) less painful, difficult, or severe.

**benevolent**—kind and generous.

**parameter**—a rule or limit that controls what something is or how something should be done.

**proponent**—a person who argues for or supports something.

**terminal illness**—an active and progressive illness for which there is no cure and the patient is expected to die within a relatively short time.

*In 2011, the well-known actor Patrick Stewart came out publicly in support of a British group that was advocating for "right to die" legislation. "I have the strong feeling that, should the time come for me, having had no role in my birth, I would like there to be a choice I might make about how I die,"*

In this way, even normally *benevolent* efforts to keep someone alive may be seen as a form of cruelty.

## Dignity in Death

Some people, like Petta in the story at the beginning of this book, suffer from what is called a progressive degenerative illness. These are illnesses, such as AIDS, Huntington's disease, and multiple sclerosis, in which a patient's condition will get worse and worse over time. Patients with a progressive degenerative disease often experience a gradual but persistent loss of

# MULTIPLE SCLEROSIS

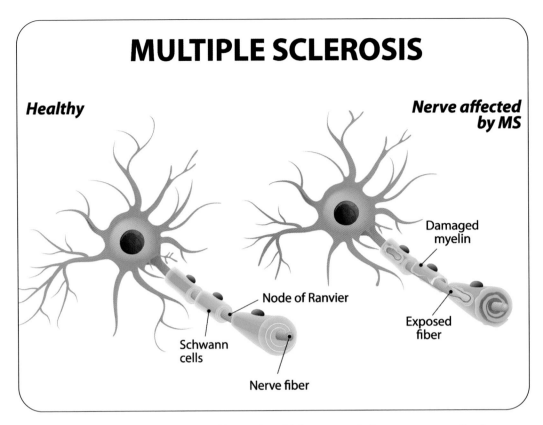

**Healthy**

**Nerve affected by MS**

Damaged myelin

Node of Ranvier

Exposed fiber

Schwann cells

Nerve fiber

*Multiple sclerosis is a degenerative disease in which a person's immune system begins to attack the central nervous system—the brain, spinal cord, and optic nerves. The disorder can cause blindness, muscle weakness, and problems with coordination that can confine the worst cases to a wheelchair, and there is no cure. Such debilitating illnesses can lead sufferers to consider ending their lives through assisted suicide.*

quality of life. They may lose the ability to move, communicate, and be independent and must rely on constant care for all of their bodily functions. For some, the loss of personal dignity is great, and they fear that the worst is yet to come, including the possibility of becoming unconscious for the rest of their lives. Should life be about quantity or quality? Proponents claim that this is about the right to die with dignity.

# Unnatural Death and Life

Euthanasia brings a life to an end before natural means have run their course. For some people, this is not as nature intended, and this is why it should be considered morally wrong and illegal. Yet there is a case to say that the time has passed when we lived our lives as nature intended. Humankind first flourished as nomadic groups of people roaming the land, hunting and gathering food. Today, hundreds of millions live in giant towns and cities. Medical advances have transformed people's lives, sustaining people that in the past would have died at a far younger age. One can say life is no longer natural as it is, and

 **Anthony Bland**

Seventeen-year-old Anthony Bland went to watch a soccer semifinal in 1989 at the Hillsborough Stadium in Sheffield, UK, when disaster struck. When police opened stadium gates to *alleviate* overcrowding, a human stampede crushed people against the fences, resulting in 96 deaths and 766 fans injured. In the chaos, Anthony suffered a severely crushed chest, which led to brain damage. Despite intense medical efforts, he lapsed into a permanent vegetative state. His parents believed their son would not have wanted to be kept alive in such a state, and they were supported by doctors at Airedale Hospital where he was being treated. After a lengthy court battle, doctors were allowed to withdraw water and artificial nutrition to hasten his death.

if this is the case, there should be nothing wrong with ending lives unnaturally as well.

## Proper Regulation of Euthanasia

Many supporters of euthanasia believe that it is not that different from many other medical practices and vital decisions made by doctors every day. All other important medical practices are controlled, so why should euthanasia be any different?

It can be regulated, many argue, provided it is first made legal in a country. It is a known fact that euthanasia and physician-assisted suicide occur in places where they are against the law. These cases often go unreported and cannot be assessed or checked. By making euthanasia legal, it would come under the control of the medical profession so that it could be monitored, performed correctly, and be made to adhere to a strict list of *parameters*.

 # Good Life, Good Death

Pioneering heart surgeon Christiaan Barnard wrote in his pro-euthanasia book, *Good Life, Good Death*: "The prime goal of medicine is to alleviate suffering and not to prolong life. . . . I have never seen any nobility in a patient's thrashing around all night in a sweat-soaked bed, trying to escape from the pain that torments him day and night. . . . To my mind, when the terminally ill patient has reached this stage, the best medical treatment is death."

Euthanasia and assisted suicide are practiced under the law in just a handful of countries throughout the world. Supporters of euthanasia argue that in these countries, there has been no massive increase in the numbers of people rushing to die.

In 1997, Oregon became the first US state to make physician-assisted suicide legal. From 1998 to 2015, 991 people have asked for and received physician-assisted suicide. In each case, strict guidelines and safeguards were followed to prevent misuse of the law and to make sure that the person communicated clearly and repeatedly their desire to end their life. In most of these cases, a patient and their medical records were carefully

*The US government challenged Oregon's Death with Dignity Act, attempting to overturn the law. In 2006, the US Supreme Court ruled in* **Gonzales v. Oregon** *that the federal government could not overrule state laws determining what constituted the appropriate use of medications that were not themselves prohibited.*

*In 2014 British entrepreneur Sir Richard Branson publicly supported right-to-die legislation that had been introduced in Parliament. The bill would have allowed doctors to prescribe a lethal dose of drugs to terminally ill patients judged to have less than six months to live. "An assisted dying law would not result in more people dying, but in fewer people suffering," Branson wrote. "Watching a loved one suffer over a long and drawn-out period can be utterly devastating. However, this isn't about relatives of loved ones making the decision. It's about those who are terminally ill but still mentally capable making the decisions about their own life and death."*

analyzed and second medical opinions sought before any action was taken. There was often a "cooling off" period in which the patient could change their mind.

A landmark court case in the euthanasia debate occurred in 1976. Karen Ann Quinlan laid unconscious in a coma and was dependent on a mechanical respirator for her survival. Her parents asked doctors to remove the respirator and let Karen die a natural death. The doctors refused, and the case went to court. The Quinlans were successful in persuading the court that the doctors' actions infringed on the patient's rights to refuse medical treatment. In agreeing with Karen's parents, the court decided that the rights of the patient overruled medical ethics. In a twist of fate, however, when Karen was removed from the respirator, she continued to breathe and remained in a coma for nearly 10 years before dying from pneumonia in 1985.

## Patients Who Are Unable to Choose

The right to choose is considered a crucial part of the argument for euthanasia and assisted suicide, but for some people, this is not an option. Some suffer severe brain injury through an accident or illness. They can fall into a deep coma, which can last a few weeks, and then pass into a state in which doctors and specialists can find no sign of upper brain activity—the part of the brain where it is believed consciousness, thinking, communication, and understanding occur. This is called a persistent vegetative state (PVS), and with life-support machines, it is possible to keep a patient in a PVS alive for many years. However, many people wonder whether it is right to do so, believing that if the parents and family members agree, euthanasia should be an option in such cases.

## Public Opinion on Euthanasia

Many opinion polls taken in a number of countries indicate that the majority of the public supports euthanasia or assisted

# American Attitudes Toward Physician-Assisted Suicide

Question: When a person has a disease that cannot be cured and is living in severe pain, do you think doctors should or should not be allowed by law to assist the patient to commit suicide if the patient requests it?

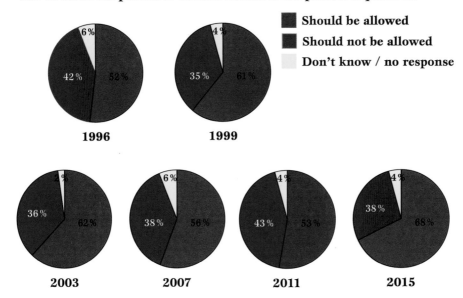

- ■ Should be allowed
- ■ Should not be allowed
- ☐ Don't know / no response

**1996:** 6%, 42%, 52%

**1999:** 4%, 35%, 61%

**2003:** 4%, 36%, 62%

**2007:** 6%, 38%, 56%

**2011:** 4%, 43%, 53%

**2015:** 4%, 38%, 68%

Source: The Gallup Organization
http://www.gallup.com/poll/183425/support-doctor-assisted-suicide.aspx

suicide in certain clearly-defined cases. In the US, for example, opinion polls show that support for legalizing voluntary euthanasia grew from 36 percent in 1950 to 61 percent in 1999; in 2014, support rose again to 69 percent.

As stated previously, religion is a strong factor in the debate. Of people in the US who attended church services weekly in 2014, only 48 percent supported euthanasia; of those who attended services less than weekly to monthly, 74 percent were in favor; and 82 percent of those who attended services less than monthly supported euthanasia.

On the issue of physician-assisted suicide, a 2015 Gallup poll showed 68 percent of US adults were in favor if the patient was terminally ill, living in severe pain, and requesting to die. This represented a 10 percent increase from the previous year. By age group, 81 percent of 18 to 34-year-olds, 65 percent of 35 to 54-year-olds, and 61 percent of those 55 and older approved of physician-assisted suicide in 2015. Politically, 61 percent of Republicans were in support, compared to 72 percent of Democrats and 80 percent of Independents.

 # Text-Dependent Questions

1. How would supporters of euthanasia respond to the claim that if euthanasia were legalized, it would be too difficult to regulate?
2. Give evidence of the differences in people's views on euthanasia based on age group.

 # Research Project

Using the Internet or your school library, research the topic of euthanasia for people in a persistent vegetative state, and answer the following question: "Should euthanasia be an option for people in a persistent vegetative state (PVS)?"

Some think that euthanasia should be an option because a person in a genuine PVS has no chance of recovery. They are technically alive, but what sort of life is it when they are not aware of anything around them? Should the parents of PVS victims have to go through many years of grief without an end? There is no quality of life, just quantity of life. Others say euthanasia should not be allowed for people in a persistent vegetative state because a person in a PVS is still a person with a right to life, no matter what their condition. There have been a number of cases where someone thought to be in a persistent vegetative state came out of that state. While there is hope of recovery or the development of a cure, it is simply unacceptable to terminate life.

Write a two-page report, using data you have found in your research to support your conclusion, and present it to your class.

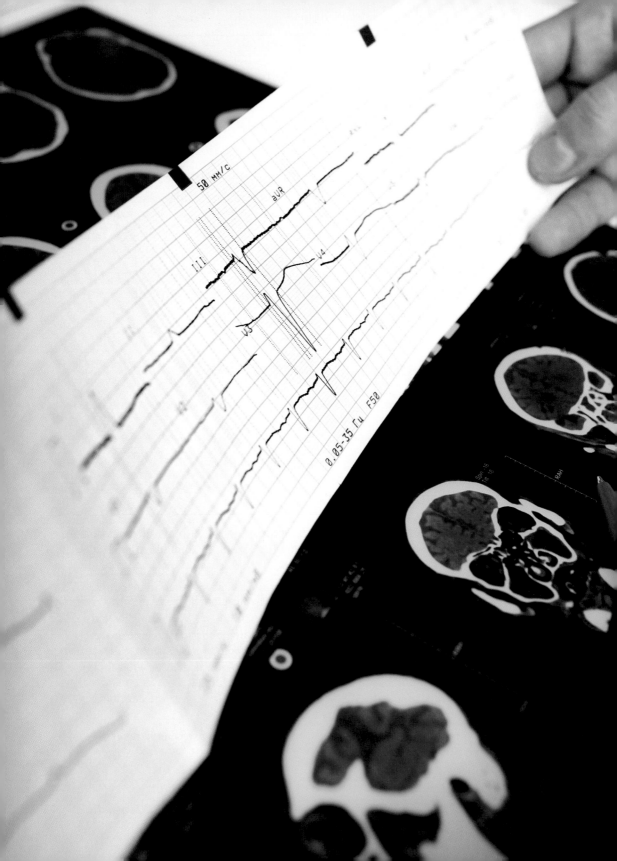

*4*

# The Arguments against Euthanasia

O pponents to euthanasia come from all walks of life, and their reasons for opposing euthanasia are just as varied. For example, some feel that legalizing it would be the start of an increasing disregard for life, while others fear it would create pressure on severely ill and elderly people to end their lives.

Euthanasia is often portrayed as the only alternative to suffering a painful, undignified death, but many say this is far from the truth. They argue that advances in painkilling techniques and drugs mean that in many more cases than in the past, patients can be given a peaceful and painless final period of their lives.

Critics also state that euthanasia does not always offer a

*One of the most important developments in health care in recent years is the growing emphasis that insurance companies place on doctors to contain costs. Some critics of euthanasia fear that it could become a means of cost containment, eliminating the terminally ill or elderly so that resources could be spent on patients with a better long-term chance of survival.*

good, easy, or dignified death. On occasion, *complications* happen. In some cases, for instance, people have been known to react to a lethal injection with violent shakes of their body and muscles. These give anything but the appearance of a calm and peaceful death and can cause great distress to friends and family who may be present at the time.

## Pain Not Motivating Physician-Assisted Suicides

Campaigners against euthanasia point out that it is not true that most patients seeking physician-assisted suicide are in excruciating pain. A *New York Times* article documented only 22 percent of patients who requested physician-assisted suicide were in pain or afraid of being in pain. Of the seven who received euthanasia in Australia when it was legal in the 1990s, three reported no pain, and the pain of the other four was controlled by medications. Most patients report the desire

 **Words to Understand in This Chapter**

**complication**—a disease or condition that happens in addition to another disease or condition: a problem that makes a disease or condition more dangerous or harder to treat.

**diagnose**—to recognize (a disease, illness, etc.) by examining someone.

**postmortem**—happening after death.

**sanctity**—the quality or state of being holy, very important, or valuable.

**unscrupulous**—not honest or fair: doing things that are wrong, dishonest, or illegal.

*Physician-assisted suicide directly conflicts with the Hippocratic Oath, which proclaims: "I will keep [the sick] from harm and injustice. I will neither give a deadly drug to anybody who asked for it, nor will I make a suggestion to this effect."*

to escape not from physical pain, but emotional distress due to depression, hopelessness, or the loss of independence.

## Complications in Physician-Assisted Suicides

Contrary to many people's beliefs, physician-assisted suicide is not a guaranteed quick and painless death, and there are tremendous consequences for those who have complications (problems that occur in addition to a disease or condition).

Euthanasia opponents say any medical procedure has a chance of complications, but the consequences are much more damaging when it is at the end of someone's life because of their physical and emotional frailty. Patients may vomit up the pills they take, not take enough pills, or even wake up instead of dying.

A 2005 study by Dutch researchers followed 138 terminally ill cancer patients and found that 7 percent vomited up the medications they took that were supposed to end their life. In 15 percent of cases, the patient did not die or took a longer time to die than expected. In 18 percent, doctors had to intervene and administer a lethal injection themselves because the pills the patient took did not work.

##  Euthanasia in the United States

In the United States, anti-euthanasia campaigners rally in multiple cities to protest against this practice. Here, powerful pressure groups on both sides of the issue are locked in a battle to try to win the full support of the public and the government. Currently, there are no laws at the federal level on euthanasia or assisted suicide. On the state level, active euthanasia is illegal in all 50 US states, but passive euthanasia is legal. For assisted suicide—in which another person provides the means of death but does not initiate the final act that ends life—there is more allowance: 45 states consider assisted suicide illegal, and five states have legalized it.

*A disabled athlete takes part in the biathalon event at the 2014 Winter Paralympics in Sochi, Russia. Despite their conditions, disabled athletes are able to live complete lives, and compete in sports at the highest levels.*

*This stained glass window in a Belgian church shows the Old Testament figure Moses presenting the Ten Commandments he received from God. These included the prohibition against taking the life of another person.*

In Oregon, 24 out of 991 physician-assisted suicide attempts included vomiting of the medications, six regained consciousness after ingesting the medications, and three had other complications.

## Religious Teachings on Euthanasia

Many religions hold that human life is sacred and granted by God or some other force higher than human beings. This viewpoint is found in the teachings of many of the world's major religions, including the Christian, Jewish, and Islamic faiths. In the Christian Bible, for instance, "Thou shall not kill" is one of God's Ten Commandments, while the holy book of Islam, the Qur'an, instructs Muslims to "Destroy not yourselves. Surely Allah is ever merciful to you." Dr. Rachamin Melamed-Cohen wrote in 2002 that, "The message of Judaism is that one must struggle until the last breath of life. Until the last moment, one has to live and rejoice and give thanks to the Creator."

Some religions even believe that suffering is a part of life

*Pope Francis, leader of the Roman Catholic Church, has denounced the right to die movement. The pope has said it is a "false sense of compassion" to consider euthanasia as an act of dignity, because Church teachings regard it as a sin against God and creation.*

and may cleanse a person or bring them closer to God. For example, the Roman Catholic leader Pope John Paul II, stated, "It is suffering, more than anything else, which clears the way for the grace which transforms human souls."

## Changing Views on Ending Life

There have been a number of occasions where people who considered euthanasia or assisted suicide went on to succeed and lead happy, worthwhile lives. A Canadian medical study of 168 terminally ill cancer patients published in the medical journal *The Lancet* showed that many patients frequently changed their minds about whether they wanted to live or die. *The Guardian* reported that in Oregon, just over a third of people since 1998 changed their minds or chose to extend their life after initially requesting a lethal prescription. Anti-euthanasia groups fear that patients could have asked for death when they were at an extremely low emotional point. If they had waited

 **Error in Judgment**

A pathologist in Australia says a woman who took her own life because she thought she had cancer did not have the disease when she died. A *postmortem* examination found evidence that Nancy Crick had suffered from previous bouts of cancer, but these had been cleared up by surgery. The 69-year-old took her own life with an overdose of drugs surrounded by supporters and euthanasia activists.

*Even patients with terminal, painful conditions such as cancer experience moments of joy despite their situations.*

even a few days, they may have made a completely different decision, but euthanasia does not allow a second chance at that choice.

## Mistakes in Diagnosis

Medical science may have advanced greatly, but much is still unknown about the human body and how it works. Some patients recover miraculously, while others are victims of honest mistakes in diagnosing, or determining, their condition. A 2008 *Live Science* article explains that accurate diagnosis, oftentimes more than treatment, is the difference between life and death because a bleak outlook can lead to reduced treatment; it can also prompt doctors or family members to remove a patient from life support.

A coma is a period of "sleep" after brain damage lasting no more than a few weeks. From the coma, a patient moves to one of three states: death, waking up with varying extents of brain damage, or moving into a vegetative state. In a vegetative state, there is minimal to no consciousness—they may be unaware of their surroundings and have little chance of improvement. However, if there is at least some consciousness, patients can recover more consciousness over time, even years later. If they are in a persistent vegetative state with no consciousness, hope becomes dire.

> "Nothing and no one can in any way permit the killing of an innocent human being."
>
> —Roman Catholic Pope John Paul II, 1980

In 2003, Terry Wallis awoke after 19 years in a vegetative state with minimal consciousness. There are many stories of patients who come out of such a state, which makes it critical to correctly *diagnose* whether someone is in a vegetative state with consciousness or in a persistent vegetative state (PVS). A study conducted in London in the 1990s revealed about a third of patients thought to be in a PVS actually showed signs of consciousness when closely examined.

Temptation to choose euthanasia can be strong for people in various situations with an inaccurate diagnosis: a family who thinks their loved one is in a PVS, a patient believing they

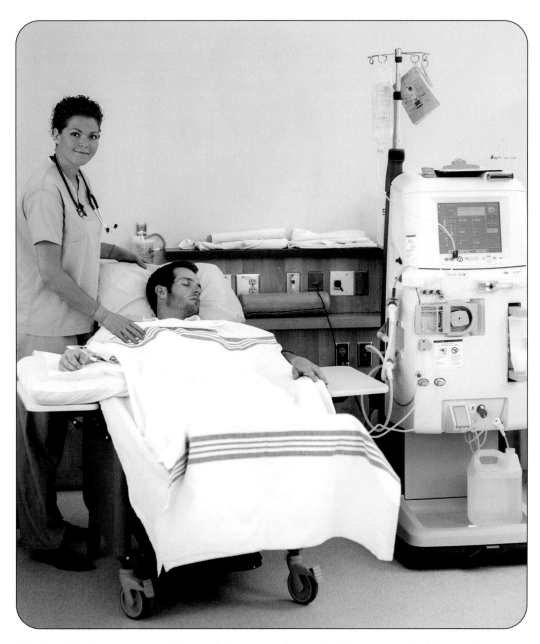

*With medical resources and drugs being expensive and ultimately limited in supply, many seriously ill people feel that they are a financial as well as an emotional burden to the people around them. Those who opposed the right to die movement fear that such feelings can be taken advantage of by euthanasia supporters.*

*Most doctors are opposed to the idea of euthanasia, as it is contrary to their goal of keeping patients alive and healthy for as long as possible.*

had no hope of a cure, or someone who believed they had just weeks to live. Perhaps the loved one is not in a persistent vegetative state but has some consciousness; a patient may actually have a different disease that has a cure; or someone may discover they have years, not weeks, to live. If euthanasia was legal, anti-euthanasia activists argue, how many of these people would die unnecessarily?

# Euthanasia "Incompatible" with Healers

The American Medical Association (AMA) became the first national professional medical association in the world in 1847, dedicating itself to "establishing standards for professional education, training, and conduct" and adopting the first national code of ethics in medicine.

The AMA's official view is that "Euthanasia is fundamentally incompatible with the physician's role as healer, would be difficult or impossible to control, and would pose serious societal risks. . . . Instead of engaging in euthanasia, physicians must aggressively respond to the needs of patients at the end of life. Patients should not be abandoned once it is determined that cure is impossible. Patients near the end of life must continue to receive emotional support, comfort care, adequate pain control, respect for patient autonomy, and good communication."

Following this stance, many doctors are opposed to euthanasia, and a key reason is the fear that trust in the medical profession would dwindle as a result of euthanasia being made legal. Would the option of euthanasia start to mean that less care and attention was paid by doctors to terminally ill people as a result? Would research into finding new techniques to care for the terminally ill or to find cures start to decline? For many anti-euthanasia groups, these are worrying possibili-

 "A society that believes in nothing can offer no argument even against death. A culture that has lost its faith in life cannot comprehend why it should be endured."

—Canadian writer Andrew Coyne

ties that could actually happen or at least raise doubts in people's minds that would reduce their trust in doctors.

## Unscrupulous Practitioners

Critics of euthanasia fear that making it legal would make ending one's life commonplace and more acceptable in society. This, they argue, could lead to a number of problems, including the authorities not investigating cases where bad medical practice has taken place. They also wonder if it would be possible to police euthanasia and monitor if *unscrupulous*, unethical practitioners had taken lives. After all, the key witness, the patient, would be dead and unable to testify.

## Right to Die versus Duty to Die

As countries' populations are now growing older and older, the proportion of nations' budgets spent on health care and other facilities for seniors who are sick is rising dramatically. In the United States, health care is no longer provided freely without thought; major decisions have to be made on the basis of cost, and not all treatments are available to all patients. Keeping someone alive in an intensive care unit costs tens of thousands of dollars. In some countries, families have to bear a portion of this great cost. Euthanasia, in contrast, is cheap and final.

With financial pressures increasing, euthanasia opponents fear that pressure will mount on doctors to suggest and perform euthanasia on people who are dying of incurable illnesses in order to save resources for patients who have a greater chance of survival.

Studies have shown how a large number of extremely eld-

*Physician-assisted suicide disproportionately affects the poor and people living with disabilities. The cost of the drugs used in physician-assisted suicide is much lower than the cost of long-term care for disabled or terminally ill people. That explains, at least in part, why there is widespread opposition from most disability rights group, including the National Council on Disability, the American Association of People with Disabilities (AAPD), the National Council on Independent Living (NCIL), the National Spinal Cord Injury Association, the World Institute on Disability and FREED.*

"Even putting aside the Judeo-Christian morality upon which the Constitution and our nation's culture are based, the notion of forced euthanasia would contradict the long-held body of medical ethics to which all American doctors must adhere."

—Surgeon and writer Sherwin B. Nuland, author of *How We Die: Reflections on Life's Final Chapter*

erly or severely ill people view themselves as a burden on their families and on society. With rising health care costs, would they feel a duty to agree to voluntary euthanasia to stop themselves from being a burden? Many believe that the right to die, far from becoming one of many options a patient can consider, could become a duty to die. Their concern is that it would be impossible to protect patients from pressure to "do the right thing."

Reuters reported that according to a UK survey of 986 doctors by Right to Life, 74 percent of them would refuse to help a patient die, while 56 percent believed it would be impossible to set clear rules for legal euthanasia. Almost half said they were concerned about being pressured by families and colleagues. Assisted suicide carries a maximum prison sentence of 14 years in the UK.

## The Sanctity of Life

Could legalizing voluntary euthanasia be the start of a slippery slope toward doctors having the power to take life without a patient's consent? That is the concern of many anti-euthanasia campaigners, some of whom point to the nightmare of Nazi Germany's T4 program. They fear that involuntary euthanasia could end up being practiced on those with severe disabilities, babies with major birth defects, **and** seniors who are not threatened with a terminal illness.

If not as extreme as the T4 program, a cultural shift could happen in which there is a lessened *sanctity*, or value, of life in society—especially on the lives of the vulnerable—with a greater tendency to suggest that **an early death** is suitable for them. Disability groups, including the Euthanasia Prevention Coalition and Not Dead Yet, are **campaigning** fiercely against euthanasia and point out that **many people** with extreme illness or disabilities continue to live lives which, although difficult, are still rewarding and worthwhile.

 # Text-Dependent Questions

1. What is the difference between **a vegetative state** and a persistent vegetative state? How does diagnosing the correct state affect a patient's outlook?
2. What are three reasons people **campaign against euthanasia?**

 # Research Project

Using the Internet or your school library, research the topic of religion and euthanasia, and answer the following question: "Should religious arguments be considered in the debate on euthanasia?"

Some contend that religious arguments on euthanasia should be considered. Religions are the ultimate code of conduct and show ways to live life that are followed by billions of people. Most religions have a similar set of morals, and they have been beneficial to societies for thousands of years. If people followed religious guidance more, there would be better treatment of one another and a greater sanctity of life. The most vulnerable people would be treated equally to the most privileged people. Others argue that religious documents such as the Bible were written such a long time ago that they are no longer relevant in deciding important issues. Religions were founded long before medical science had reached its current state, so they cannot speak to what is going on today.

Write a two-page report, using data you have found in your research to support your conclusion, and present it to your class.

# 5

# Places Where Euthanasia Is Legal

Euthanasia and assisted suicide have been performed in many places around the world, but they are only legal in a handful of states and countries: in the Netherlands, Belgium, Switzerland, Luxembourg, Colombia, and five US states, laws allow certain cases of voluntary euthanasia or assisted suicide to take place; Canada is currently in the process of making them legal.

Euthanasia and assisted suicide had occurred in the Netherlands without court interference since the 1980s, but in 2002, the Dutch government passed a new law making them officially legal. The Netherlands became the first country to legalize euthanasia nationwide. In 2002, the official figures state that there were 1,882 cases of euthanasia, the majority of which were of people suffering from cancer.

*In the Netherlands, assisted suicide is legal—and not just for those with terminal illnesses. Holland's 2002 Termination of Life on Request and Assisted Suicide Act allows doctors to perform euthanasia on anyone with "unbearable suffering." This goes beyond terminal illnesses to include dementia, mental illnesses, and illnesses for which there is no available and suitable treatment.*

Belgium also passed a law legalizing euthanasia and assisted suicide in 2002, shortly after its Dutch neighbors. Patients there must make repeated, voluntary requests to die, be assessed by two separate doctors, and wait a month between the written request and the action; a psychologist must take part if the competency of the patient is in doubt. In its first year of operation in Belgium, more than 200 cases of euthanasia and assisted suicide were estimated to have occurred.

## The First Place to Legalize Euthanasia

The Northern Territory in Australia became the first place in the world to make voluntary euthanasia fully legal in 1996. Under this law, two doctors had to confirm that a patient was terminally ill and suffering unbearable pain. A psychiatrist also had to declare that the patient was not suffering from depression that could be treated.

Bob Dent, a terminally ill cancer patient, was the first to die under the 1996 law. The lethal injection was administered by a computer, using software developed by Dr. Philip Nitschke, a leading "right to die" campaigner. To operate it, the patient had

 **Words to Understand in This Chapter**

**autopsy**—an examination of a dead body to find out the cause of death.

**coroner**—a public official whose job is to find out the cause of death when people die in ways that are violent, sudden, etc.

to answer a series of questions, the final one asking if they wanted to die. If the patient answered "yes," the machine would deliver a fatal dose of drugs. Only four people died under the law before it was over-turned in 1998.

## Jack Kevorkian, "Dr. Death"

American doctor Jack Kevorkian was possibly the world's most famous *proponent* of assisted suicide. In the late 1980s, Dr. Kevorkian built a machine that helped people commit suicide by giving them a lethal dose of potassium chloride. In 1990, this machine

*Dr. Philip Nitschke has developed several instruments for aiding in euthanasia and assisted suicide cases.*

helped Janet Adkins die in the state of Michigan. She was the first of over 130 people that Dr. Kevorkian helped to kill themselves in assisted suicide cases. Dr. Kevorkian lost his medical license along with access to lethal drugs in the early 1990s. He switched to using the poisonous gas carbon monoxide and was tried for crimes four times without being convicted.

Nicknamed "Dr. Death," Kevorkian stepped up his right-to-death campaign by giving a lethal injection to Thomas Youk in 1998. This action was videotaped and broadcast on US television, provoking great debate. In 1999, Kevorkian was found guilty of second-degree murder and imprisoned for eight years.

# US States that Permit Euthanasia

The state of Oregon introduced the Death with Dignity Act in 1994, allowing physician-assisted suicide for the first time in the US, but legal challenges held the law back from implementation until late 1997. The Death with Dignity Act outlaws euthanasia but allows physician-assisted suicide under the following restrictions: the patient must make two spoken requests and one written request before a witness and be terminally ill with less than six months to live. Patients must convince two doctors that their decision is definite and must not be influenced by depression. They are then given a prescription dose of lethal drugs, which they must administer themselves. In the period 1998 to 2015, 991 registered deaths in Oregon were a result of physician-assisted suicide under the Death with Dignity Act.

Similar to neighboring countries Belgium and the Netherlands, the US state of Washington was the second state to legalize physician-assisted suicide in 2008 after its neighbor Oregon was the first state to do so. Washington's law is also

*Dr. Jack Kevorkian became internationally known for publicly supporting the right of terminally ill patients to end their lives. He claimed to have assisted at least 130 patients to that end. An American court convicted Kevorkian of second-degree murder after he participated in a suicide, and he spent eight years in prison. Kevorkian died in 2011.*

# Key Conditions of Dutch Law

According to a 2015 BBC News article, the rate of euthanasia in the Netherlands has remained fairly stable at 2.8 percent of all deaths. There is a set of conditions that must be met before euthanasia can be performed:

- The patient's suffering must be unbearable, with no hope of improvement.
- The patient is not required to have a terminal illness and is not limited to physical suffering. It can include emotional distress such as the prospect of losing personal dignity, a worsening condition, or the fear of suffocation.

Only the Netherlands and Belgium permit euthanasia for patients under the age of 18. In the Netherlands, a patient may request euthanasia or assisted suicide if they are mentally competent and age 16 or older. A parent or guardian cannot overrule the patient's decision but must be consulted. Competent patients between 12 and 16 years old may also qualify but only if their parent or guardian consents. A second doctor must see the patient to confirm their request is valid and their suffering unbearable; there is a network of doctors trained to make these consultations.

In terms of regulation, a doctor must report the case to the *coroner*, who passes it to a regional committee. If the committee finds the doctor did not follow the legal requirements, the case is referred to the prosecution service and to the body that regulates doctors.

# The Situation in Switzerland

Under article 115 of the 1942 Swiss penal code, it is a crime to help a person commit suicide out of "self-seeking" motives, such as receiving money. This has been taken to mean that as long as the motives are unselfish, assisted suicide is not a crime.

Dignitas is one of several Swiss groups that assists in suicides. It has performed more than 1,000 since the group's formation in 1998. Applicants, who must be over 18, fill out forms, provide medical records proving they are terminally ill, severely disabled, or in unbearable pain, and are then interviewed by Dignitas and a Swiss doctor to discuss their case. If

approved, patients are given a lethal dose of drugs to take either at home or in an apartment rented by Dignitas in the Swiss city of Zurich. The patient is again asked if they are sure of their decision; many people have changed their minds at this stage. If they go ahead with the procedure, they are usually asleep within five minutes before falling into a coma and then dying. The police are alerted and then carry out a routine investigation.

called the Death with Dignity Act and follows similar guidelines, but the patient must make their requests for death at least 15 days apart. After Washington, three other states legalized physician-assisted suicide in the US: Montana in 2009, Vermont in 2013, and California in 2015. Four states— Nevada, North Carolina, Utah, and Wyoming—do not have clear laws either way on the legality of assisted suicide.

> "People want the right to die at a time of their own choosing. Too many families have watched helplessly as a relative dies slowly, longing for death."
>
> —British journalist Polly Toynbee

## Illegal Euthanasia Cases

There have been a number of instances where euthanasia and assisted suicide have occurred in countries that do not permit them. In some nations, like the Netherlands before its 2002 law, the authorities tended not to prosecute those who committed euthanasia or assisted in a suicide.

In many other nations, people have been convicted and imprisoned for their actions. In 2001, after many years of legal battles, Canada's highest court ordered the imprisonment of Robert Latimer for the 1993 murder of his daughter, Tracy, who had a disability. Latimer argued that he had suffocated his daughter out of love and necessity because she was in great pain from her severe cerebral palsy.

Another case involved the death in 1998 of George Liddell, an 85-year-old terminally ill cancer patient. His physician, Dr. David Moor, admitted to giving Mr. Liddell a dose of painkillers to ease pain, which eventually killed him.

In 2008, retired French teacher Chantal Sebire was diagnosed with a rare form of cancer and refused treatment, requesting death through euthanasia instead. It is illegal in France, so her request was denied by the French court. Sebire was found dead a few days later. The *autopsy* concluded that she did not die of natural causes but of a toxin used in physician-assisted suicides in other countries—one that is not available in French pharmacies.

## Suicide Tourism

Suicide tourism is when people travel from a country that outlaws euthanasia and assisted suicide to another country that permits them in order to die. In January 2003, for example, Englishman Reginald Crew traveled with his wife to

 **Hungarian Nurse Imprisoned**

The *International Herald Tribune* reported that 24-year-old Timea Faludi was sentenced to nine years in prison and banned from nursing for life after being found guilty of the murder of an elderly patient and the attempted killing of six others to relieve them of their pain and suffering. She originally confessed to killing approximately 40 patients but later retracted this confession. Euthanasia is illegal in Hungary and hospitals are conducting investigations into how deaths are reported.

*Euthanasia is legal in Belgium for adults who have terminal conditions that cause a person chronic pain.*

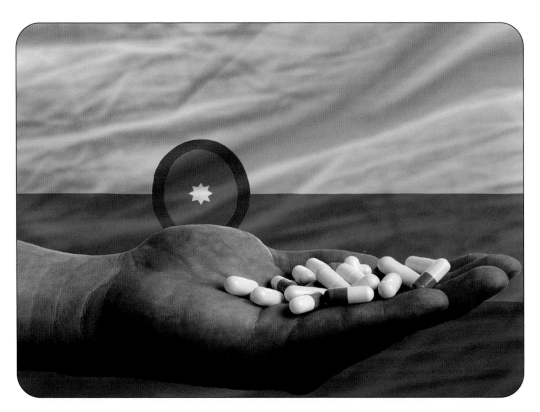

*The South American country of Colombia permits euthanasia, although many of the country's Roman Catholic citizens oppose this practice on religious grounds. In 2015 Colombia's government set out guidelines for doctors to follow in euthanasia cases.*

Switzerland, where he died from an assisted suicide. In 2000, three foreigners traveled to Switzerland to die, but by 2002, that number had risen to 58. Between 2008 and 2012, 611 people from 31 countries came to Switzerland for assisted suicide. The majority were from Europe, with 44 percent from Germany and 21 percent from the UK; 21 total people were from the US.

Some fear a flood of hundreds, maybe thousands, of people seeking an early death. Euthanasia supporters, however, feel that this is scare-mongering since Switzerland is alone in allowing nonresidents assisted suicide. They say many patients who would like an early death are no longer in a suitable condition to travel, so a flood of suicide tourists to Switzerland is not a realistic worry.

 # Text-Dependent Questions

1. What conditions must be met before euthanasia can be performed in the Netherlands?
2. In which US states is physician-assisted suicide legal, and in what years did their laws pass?

 # Research Project

Using the Internet or your school library, research the topic of suicide tourism, and answer the following question: "Should suicide tourism be outlawed?"

Some believe that it should be outlawed because people are traveling to another country specifically to have euthanasia or assisted suicide performed. People should have to obey the laws of their country of citizenship, including end of life procedures. They have lived in their home country their whole lives and enjoyed all its benefits, so a citizen's responsibility is to abide by its laws in return. If they want euthanasia or assisted suicide in another country where it is legal, they should have to become citizens of that new country first.

Others maintain that suicide tourism should not be outlawed. A person has to follow and live by the laws of a country they visit during their stay there, whether it is about the speed limit, robbery, or anything else. If someone wants to die by euthanasia or assisted suicide and chooses to go to a foreign country to do so, they should be able to do what they want if it is allowed in that country.

Write a two-page report, using data you have found in your research to support your conclusion, and present it to your class.

# 6

# Society's Views on Older People

In many wealthy countries, most people retire when they reach age 60 or 65. They receive a *pension* from the government or their employer, or they live on money saved while they were at work. But should they have the right to keep working if they want to?

Many societies traditionally value older peoples' experience and work contribution. This perspective still exists in many poor countries where people often have no choice but to work for their entire lives merely to survive. In some Western industrial societies, however, the age of a worker has become a target of discrimination.

*An elderly craftsman cuts a piece of copper in a metalsmith's workshop. Although many older people believe they should have a right to assisted suicide if they so choose, some opponents of euthanasia are concerned that older people will be targeted if it becomes widely legal. They note that after retirement senior citizens make no or little positive contribution to the economics of the country, while using a disproportionate share of health care and social service resources.*

## How Do Older Workers Suffer Discrimination?

Discrimination against older workers becomes more serious during economic crises. Companies try to save money by reducing wage payments. Since older people are likely to occupy more senior positions that pay higher wages, companies often try to lay them off first.

Outside of difficult financial times, there are also general prejudices against older workers that exist. Some employers fear that they might be less familiar with modern technology. They might be less mobile physically and have health issues. They may be less willing to adapt to fast-changing work practices or learn new skills.

But there are signs that these attitudes are changing. Companies who have deliberately recruited older workers have found that they can be particularly reliable and trustworthy. They may have emotional maturity and a wider experience of life, which can make them better at coping with problems.

Older women, who have already raised their families, are also less likely than younger female workers to need maternity

 **Words to Understand in This Chapter**

**federal**—of or relating to the central (national) government.

**pension**—an amount of money that a company or the government pays to a person who is retired or sick and no longer works.

leave. Employers who run stores say that many customers appreciate the "old-fashioned" courtesy of older staff.

## What Laws Protect Seniors?

In the United States, the Age Discrimination in Employment Act of 1967 (ADEA) forbids age discrimination against people who are age 40 or older in hiring, promotion, firing, or pay. The law is specifically against discrimination against older workers: it is not illegal for an employer to favor an older worker over a younger one, even if both are age 40 or older. Though there is no *federal* law, some states also have laws that protect younger workers from age discrimination.

 **Who Were the Gray Panthers?**

In the United States, a group of senior activists called the Gray Panthers demanded the same rights as younger people who had access to jobs and promotions. They objected to advertisements which included phrases such as "People over 50 need not apply" or "Bright, young person wanted."

The Gray Panthers took their name and many of their ideas from civil rights campaigns, especially the Black Power movement. The Panthers believed in absolute equality for all people, regardless of age, color, disability, or sex and thought that doing useful work gave meaning and purpose to everyone's life. Being denied the chance to work took these away.

The Age Discrimination Act of 1975 prohibits discrimination on the basis of age in programs and activities receiving federal financial assistance, such as government offices and public educational institutions; it applies to all ages.

 ## Text-Dependent Questions

1. What did the Gray Panthers advocate for, and where did they draw some of their ideas from?
2. What are three advantages older workers might have over their younger counterparts?

 ## Research Project

Using the Internet or your school library, research the topic of age discrimination, and answer the following question: "Should certain jobs be allowed to have an age limit?"

Some think that there should be no age limit on any job because all that matters is if the employee is able to do the work. Everyone should at least have the chance to prove themselves at a job. Others say that for some jobs, like in construction or mail delivery, there should be an age limit because of the strength or mobility requirements involved. This would prevent older workers from being in unsafe situations, and companies would be more productive.

Write a two-page report, using data you have found in your research to support your conclusion, and present it to your class.

# 7

# Trends in the Euthanasia Debate

There is no one type of person who becomes a support-er for, or a critic of, euthanasia. People of all ages from all cultures and walks of life are involved in pressure and campaign groups on both sides. In the past 30 years, the number of organizations campaigning on various aspects of the issue has increased greatly.

Dozens of pro and anti-euthanasia groups campaign by lob-bying politicians, publishing books and pamphlets, using organized action, and holding rallies, meetings, and demonstra-tions. For example, Not Dead Yet, an anti-euthanasia group in the US, has appeared outside pro-euthanasia meetings handing out leaflets. The Patients Rights Council, an anti-euthanasia group, and Dignity in Dying, a pro-euthanasia group, are just two of many organizations that maintain large websites of

*Anti-euthanasia supporters protest outside a pro-euthanasia meeting.*

information in the hope of influencing and recruiting more and more supporters.

The words and actions of patients and family members facing the euthanasia debate can carry great weight. In the US, for instance, there was a highly-publicized battle between the husband and parents of a woman with severe brain damage, Terri Schiavo, over whether she should be artificially kept alive. This prompted different right-to-life groups to join forces in order to campaign with the parents.

In contrast, one terminally ill journalist from the UK, Phil Such, attracted publicity when he went on hunger strike for a change in the law banning voluntary euthanasia. The journalist said, "I have had a great, if rather short, life. Why should this be wrecked by a long, lingering death? I am really proud of my country, yet, right at this moment, I wish to God I had been born in Holland or Oregon in the US."

# People Involved in the Campaigns

The two main sides in the euthanasia debate rarely try to get the other to change their mind. Nearly all of their campaign efforts go into influencing three groups of people: governments

 **Words to Understand in This Chapter**

**advocate**—a person who argues for or supports a cause or policy.

**palliative**—something that reduces the effects or symptoms of a medical condition without curing it.

*A 2010 protest in Dallas against the Affordable Care Act, legislation that provided health care to all Americans that was sometimes called Obamacare. Before the legislation was passed in 2009, some critics claimed that it would create "death panels" of bureaucrats who would decide whether Americans—such as senior citizens or children with genetic disorders such as Down syndrome—would receive medical care. Though this claim was quickly proven to be false, public belief in this has persisted.*

and courts which make and enforce laws, the general public, and doctors and other members of the medical profession. Doctors, particularly, face frequent lobbying and surveys from opposing groups, as both sides know that getting their support would greatly influence the public and the government.

Both sides sometimes accuse each other of not reflecting the views of the majority of the people and of being funded by

The American Medical Association (AMA), the largest and most important organization of doctors in the United States, has consistently opposed euthanasia and the practice of assisted suicide. The AMA's official policy states:

(1) Physician assisted suicide is fundamentally inconsistent with the physician's professional role.

(2) It is critical that the medical profession redouble its efforts to ensure that dying patients are provided optimal treatment for their pain and other discomfort. . . . Evaluation and treatment by a health professional with expertise in the psychiatric aspects of terminal illness can often alleviate the suffering that leads a patient to desire assisted suicide.

(3) Physicians must resist the natural tendency to withdraw physically and emotionally from their terminally ill patients.

(4) Requests for physician assisted suicide should be a signal to the physician that the patient's needs are unmet and further evaluation to identify the elements contributing to the patient's suffering is necessary.

(5) Further efforts to educate physicians about advanced pain management techniques, both at the undergraduate and graduate levels, are necessary to overcome any shortcomings in this area.

powerful special-interest groups. Pro-euthanasia *advocates* are sometimes accused of being in league with private medical companies who might see euthanasia as a way of keeping costs down. Anti-euthanasia groups are sometimes accused of being in the control of religious groups who have a wider set of beliefs than just euthanasia to promote.

# Successes of Anti-Euthanasia Groups

Members of the anti-euthanasia lobby point to the very small number of places in the world that allow euthanasia or assisted suicide as an example of their success. Attempts to pass assisted suicide laws in a number of American states, including New Hampshire and Maine, have failed, while the 1996 law allowing voluntary euthanasia and assisted suicide in the Northern Territory of Australia was overturned in 1998. After intense campaigning by the pressure group, Right to Life Australia, as well as some church leaders, the federal government passed the Andrews Bill, which reversed the law in the Northern Territory. Only four people died under the law while it was in existence.

# Successes of Pro-Euthanasia Groups

Considering the fact that euthanasia was rarely discussed in the past, simply raising awareness of the issue is heralded as a major success by many euthanasia supporters. Many also believe that it is far more difficult to change the law and the way society acts than to maintain the same laws and attitudes already in place. This is why the legalization of euthanasia or assisted suicide, albeit in only a handful of places, is still viewed by many supporters as being highly significant.

The head of the Dutch Voluntary Euthanasia Society, Dr. Rob Jonquiere, said that the Dutch law of 2002 on euthanasia and assisted suicide has given a major boost to similar efforts in other European countries: "Belgium has followed suit, Luxembourg has been busy and only missed legalization by one or two votes. We know they are busy in France and in the UK." Since that statement, Luxembourg legalized euthanasia and assisted suicide in its 2009 law, while France and the UK have not.

## An Alternative Way

In some people's view, there is an alternative to both euthanasia and keeping patients alive in intensive care units in hospi-

 **Rejected Bills in the UK**

In the summer of 2003, a new bill, introduced by Lord Joel Joffe, was debated in the UK Houses of Parliament. The bill would have allowed a terminally ill adult to ask for medical help to end their life. "This issue has been debated at length in the media and every poll in the last decade shows over 80 percent public support in favor of changing the law," said Lord Joffe. The bill was rejected by parliament, as were the three subsequent attempts by Lord Joffe to introduce the bill. Similar to the AMA, the British Medical Association has maintained a stance against assisted suicide and euthanasia, which many believe has influenced parliament.

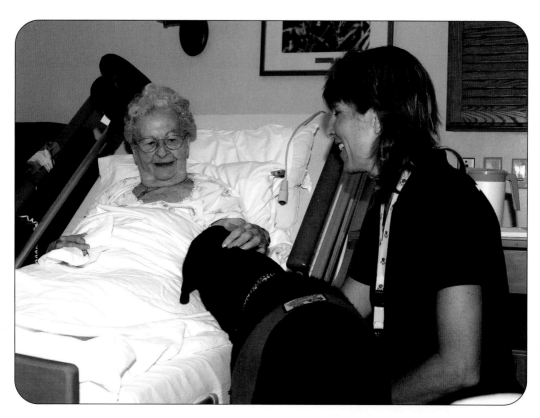

*A hospice patient enjoys interacting with a therapy dog and her gentle careworker.*

tals. Known as *palliative* care, it concentrates on caring not curing, making terminally ill patients' last days alive as comfortable as possible. This can occur in dedicated centers for the terminally ill, known as hospices, which can exist in nursing homes, care centers, or at a person's own home. Pain prevention and relief is the priority, but there is also counseling and assistance for the patient, their family, and friends.

Critics point out that this care is not available to all: there are nowhere near enough beds for all terminally ill patients, and most hospices are staffed to treat just a small number of the wide range of terminal diseases that people suffer from. In response, advocates of hospices say that this is more of an issue of financing than a fault with their kind of care.

## Vincent Humbert

At the end of 2003, France was undergoing its biggest-ever debate on euthanasia, sparked by the writings and death of Vincent Humbert. Vincent Humbert was a teenager when a car accident in 2000 left him paralyzed, mute, and blind. To write his book, he had to squeeze a journalist's palm with his right thumb, the only part of his body he could move, to select each letter of every word. *I Ask the Right to Die* immediately became

*Dame Cicely Saunders is regarded by many as the founder of modern palliative care.*

a best-seller. It was published in the same week that Marie Humbert, Vincent's mother, put an overdose of sedatives into his drip line. He died two days later.

Prosecutors charged Marie Humbert with willfully administering toxic substances to a vulnerable person, which carries a maximum five year sentence. Dr. Frederic Chaussoy, who switched off Vincent's life-support machine and also injected a lethal dose of drugs, was charged with "premeditated poisoning." In October 2003, a survey showed that 88 percent of the French population believed the laws must be changed. But many, including the French health minister, Jean-Francois Mattei, were unconvinced, and believed that the law could not resolve what was, in his opinion, "a problem of conscience." Charges against both Marie Humbert and Frederic Chaussoy were dropped by the French court in 2006, but the law remained unchanged in outlawing euthanasia and assisted suicide.

*Marie Humbert, who apparently injected sedatives into her son's drip, forcing him into a deep coma.*

# The Future of Euthanasia

No one knows for certain what will happen in the euthanasia debate in the future, but it is likely that campaigns for and against it will become even more intense.

In the US, for example, the situation in Oregon and cases like that of Terri Schiavo are sparking major discussions. Further high-profile cases of individuals in suffering who make eloquent cases for a right to choose the time and manner of their death may lead to changes in public opinion and perceptions.

On the other side, it may not take many cases of unscrupulous doctors performing involuntary euthanasia—which are proven to be against patients' wishes—or of malpractice and painful, botched killing attempts, to harden public opinion and government action against euthanasia. In addition, future advances in medical knowledge may lead to new ways of treating or even curing what were thought to be irreversible illnesses and conditions.

 **Painkilling Alternatives**

Dr. Eric Chevlen, Director of Palliative Care at St. Elizabeth Health Center in Ohio, stated, "We already know enough to manage virtually all cases of malignant pain successfully. The widely held belief that pain can be relieved only by doses of morphine so high as to render the patient a zombie is a myth."

Whatever happens, both sides will continue to monitor the situation in places that have recently decriminalized euthanasia or assisted suicide, seeking to find further arguments for their case. Whatever their differences, all sides in the euthanasia debate know that it is a complex and vital issue that is not going to go away.

 # Text-Dependent Questions

1. What types of special-interest groups are pro-euthanasia and anti-euthanasia groups accused of being influenced by, respectively?
2. Describe an alternative third way besides euthanasia or keeping someone alive in intensive care units.

 # Research Project

Using the Internet or your school library, research the topic of the pros and cons of euthanasia, and answer the following question: "Is euthanasia a way for someone to die with dignity?"

Some think that euthanasia is a dignified way to die. People have a right to say goodbye to their loved ones and to not have to die in agony. Euthanasia allows a patient to die when and where they want, at the time they choose, and in a relatively painless manner.

Others say that there is no dignity in many of the actual methods used in euthanasia, which may include inhaling gas or taking medications that may have complications. With euthanasia, the person dying is oftentimes not sure if they are making a wrong, irreversible decision. Family members may also disagree with the choice, causing greater pain in loved ones.

Write a two-page report, using data you have found in your research to support your conclusion, and present it to your class.

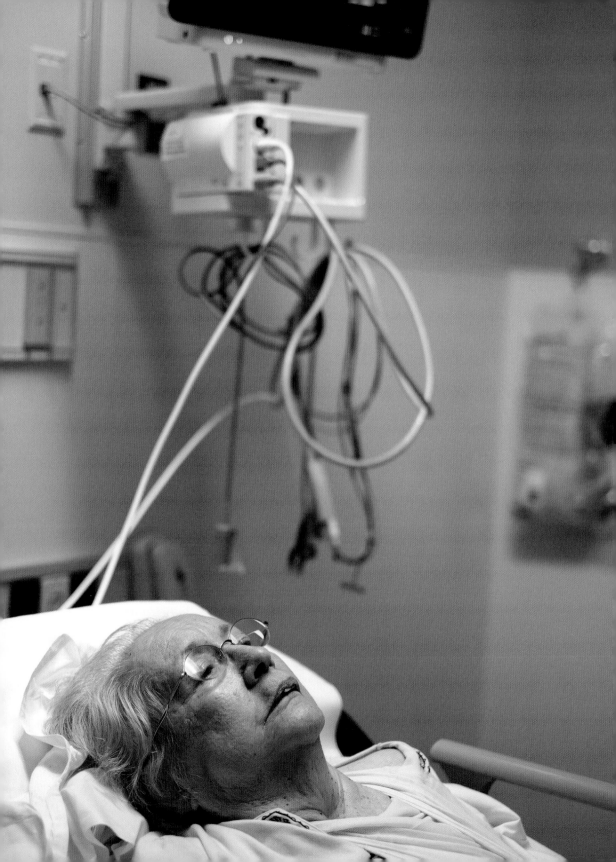

# Statistics on Euthanasia

## Selected Statistics about the Oregon Death with Dignity Act (1998-2015)

### Number of reported assisted suicide deaths
1998-2014: 859

2015: 132

Total: 991

### Number of reported lethal prescriptions written
1998-2014: 1,327

2015: 218

Total: 1,545

### Instances when health care provider was present when lethal medications were ingested by patient
1998-2014: 376

2015: 28

Total: 404

**Median age at death (range)**
    1998-2014: 71 (25-96)
    2015: 73 (30-102)
    Total: 71 (25-102)

**Deaths by gender**
    1998-2014: 453 male (52.7%), 406 female (47.3%)
    2015: 56 male (42.4%), 76 female (57.6%)
    Total: 509 male (51.4%), 482 female (48.6%)

Source: Oregon Death with Dignity Act,
2015 Data Summary

# End of Life Concerns for Patients Who Died under the Oregon Death with Dignity Act

**Less able to engage in activities making life enjoyable**
    1998-2014: 758 (88.7%)
    2015: 127 (96.2%)
    Total: 885 (89.7%)

**Losing autonomy**
    1998-2014: 782 (91.5%)
    2015: 121 (92.4%)
    Total: 903 (91.6%)

## Loss of dignity

    1998-2014: 579 (79.3%)

    2015: 98 (75.4%)

    Total: 677 (78.7%)

## Losing control of bodily functions

    1998-2014: 428 (50.1%)

    2015: 46 (35.7%)

    Total: 474 (48.2%)

## Burden on family, friends/caregivers

    1998-2014: 342 (40.0%)

    2015: 63 (48.1%)

    Total: 405 (41.1%)

## Inadequate pain control or concern about it

    1998-2014: 211 (24.7%)

    2015: 37 (28.7%)

    Total: 248 (25.2%)

## Financial implications of treatment

    1998-2014: 27 (3.2%)

    2015: 3 (2.3%)

    Total: 30 (3.1%)

Source: Oregon Death with Dignity Act,
2015 Data Summary

# Statistics on Euthanasia and Assisted Suicide in the Netherlands

**Total euthanasia or physician-assisted suicide deaths**
> 2005: 2,425
> 2010: 4,050

**Percent of all deaths due to euthanasia or physician-assisted suicide**
> 2005: 1.7%
> 2010: 2.8%

**Percent of all cases reported to a review committee**
> 2005: 80%
> 2010: 77%

**Percent of hastening of death without patient request**
> 2005: 0.8%
> 2010: 0.2%

**Percent of requests for euthanasia or physician-assisted suicide granted**
> 2005: 37%
> 2010: 45%

> Source: *The Lancet*, "Trends in end-of-life practices before and after the enactment of the euthanasia law in the Netherlands from 1990 to 2010: a repeated cross-sectional survey."

# Survey of British Doctors on Assisted Suicide

A 2009 survey of doctors in the UK—where assisted suicide is illegal—found divided opinions on assisted suicide: 39 percent were in favor of changing the law to make assisted suicide legal, 49 percent opposed a change to the law, and 12 percent did not agree or disagree. Doctors who either reported caring for the dying or professed a religious belief were less likely to support a change in the law. Gender, specialty, and years of experience had no significant effect.

Source: *BMC Medical Ethics*, Survey of doctors' opinions of the legalisation of physician assisted suicide, 2009

# Prevalence of Euthanasia and Assisted Suicide in Belgium

**Percent of all deaths due to euthanasia**
  1998: 1.1%
  2001: 0.3%
  2007: 1.9%
  2013: 4.6%

## Percent of all deaths due to assisted suicide

    1998: 0.12 %

    2001: 0.01 %

    2007: 0.07 %

    2013: 0.05 %

## Percent of all deaths with request of euthanasia or assisted suicide

    1998: 2.1 %

    2001: ——

    2007: 3.5 %

    2013: 6.0 %

## Percent of requests for euthanasia or assisted suicide granted

    1998: 57.4 %

    2001:——

    2007: 56.3 %

    2013: 76.8 %

## Percent of hastening of death without explicit request from patient

    1998: 3.2 %

    2001: 1.5 %

    2007: 1.8 %

    2013: 1.7 %

Source: *The New England Journal of Medicine,* "Recent Trends in Euthanasia and Other End-of-Life Practices in Belgium, 2015"

# Organizations to Contact

**The Arc for People
with Intellectual and Developmental Disabilities**
1825 K Street, NW, Suite 1200
Washington, DC 20006
http://www.thearc.org

**Center for Equal Opportunity**
7700 Leesburg Pike, Suite 231
Falls Church, VA 22043
http://www.ceousa.org

**Euthanasia Prevention Coalition International**
P.O. Box 611309
Port Huron, MI 48061-1309
http://www.epcc.ca

**Death with Dignity National Center**
520 SW 6th Avenue, Suite 1220
Portland, OR 97204
https://www.deathwithdignity.org

**Patients Rights Council**

PO Box 760

Steubenvilie, OH 43952

http://www.patientsrightscouncil.org/site

**Not Dead Yet**

497 State Street

Rochester, NY 14608

http://notdeadyet.org

**Christian Medical Fellowship**

6 Marshalsea Road

London SE1 1HL

United Kingdom

http://www.cmf.org.uk

# Series Glossary

**apartheid**—literally meaning "apartness," the political policies of the South African government from 1948 until the early 1990s designed to keep peoples segregated based on their color.

**BCE and CE**—alternatives to the traditional Western designation of calendar eras, which used the birth of Jesus as a dividing line. BCE stands for "Before the Common Era," and is equivalent to BC ("Before Christ"). Dates labeled CE, or "Common Era," are equivalent to *Anno Domini* (AD, or "the Year of Our Lord").

**colony**—a country or region ruled by another country.

**democracy**—a country in which the people can vote to choose those who govern them.

**detention center**—a place where people claiming asylum and refugee status are held while their case is investigated.

**ethnic cleansing**—an attempt to rid a country or region of a particular ethnic group. The term was first used to describe the attempt by Serb nationalists to rid Bosnia of Muslims.

**house arrest**—to be detained in your own home, rather than in prison, under the constant watch of police or other government forces, such as the army.

**reformist**—a person who wants to improve a country or an institution, such as the police force, by ridding it of abuses or faults.

**republic**—a country without a king or queen, such as the US.

**United Nations**—an international organization set up after the end of World War II to promote peace and co-operation throughout the world. Its predecessor was the League of Nations.

**UN Security Council**—the permanent committee of the United Nations that oversees its peacekeeping operations around the world.

**World Bank**—an international financial organization, connected to the United Nations. It is the largest source of financial aid to developing countries.

**World War I**—A war fought in Europe from 1914 to 1918, in which an alliance of nations that included Great Britain, France, Russia, Italy, and the United States defeated the alliance of Germany, Austria-Hungary, the Ottoman Empire, and Bulgaria.

**World War II**—A war fought in Europe, Africa, and Asia from 1939 to 1945, in which the Allied Powers (the United States, Great Britain, France, the Soviet Union, and China) worked together to defeat the Axis Powers (Germany, Italy, and Japan).

# Further Reading

Beville, Kieran. *Dying to Kill: A Christian Perspective on Euthanasia and Assisted Suicide.* Cambridge, Ohio: Christian Publishing House, 2014.

Butler, Katy. *Knocking on Heaven's Door: The Path to a Better Way of Death.* New York: Scribner, 2014.

Chell, Byron. *Aid in Dying The Ultimate Argument: The Clear Ethical Case for Physician Assisted Death.* North Charleston, SC: CreateSpace, 2014.

Haerens, Margaret. *Euthanasia.* Farmington Hills, Mich.: Greenhaven Press, 2015.

Prokofieff, Sergei O., and Peter Selg. *Honoring Life: Medical Ethics and Physician-Assisted Suicide.* Herndon, Va.: SteinerBooks, 2014.

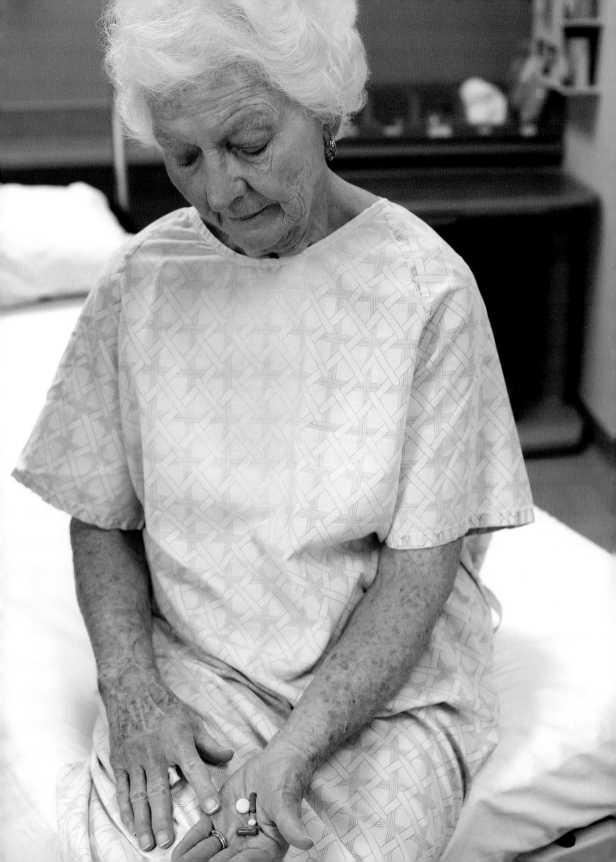

# Internet Resources

http://euthanasia.procon.org/
  A comprehensive website that provides pros and cons to euthanasia and physician-assisted suicide, including definitions, practical concerns, religious points of view, legal considerations, and historical information.

http://www.religioustolerance.org/euth_wld.htm
  A balanced website with information on the history of euthanasia, the situation in a number of countries, and the arguments for and against.

http://www.patientsrightscouncil.org/site/
  Formerly called the International Task Force on Euthanasia and Assisted Suicide, the Patients Rights Council is a US-based organization opposing euthanasia. The website contains many fact sheets and details of specific cases and campaigns.

http://www.dignityindying.org.uk/
  Campaign for assisted suicide with news, opinions, legal information, resources, and personal stories.

http://www.euthanasia.com
  Large and comprehensive website offering articles, debate topics, and cases that are presented from an anti-euthanasia perspective.

http://www.dignitas.ch/

Dignitas promotes euthanasia and has news and videos from around the world for its campaign.

http://www.epcc.ca/

The Euthanasia Prevention Coalition has newsletters, petitions, book recommendations, resources, and blogs that oppose euthanasia.

# Index

Numbers in ***bold italics*** refer to captions.